272

Stories Jesus Told

Stories Jesus Told

Norman J. Bull

Illustrations by Graham Byfield

 Augsburg Publishing House, Minneapolis

First published in Great Britain by Evans Brothers Limited, 1969
First American edition, 1969

Set in 12 on 13 point Imprint 3 point leaded and printed in Great Britain by
Cox & Wyman, Ltd., London, Fakenham and Reading

Contents

Stories Jesus told are found in the Bible. The Bible is one big book. But really it is many books, all joined together in one. All these books are made into one book because all of them are about God.

Four of these books in the Bible tell us about Jesus. They are called *Gospels* which means *Books of Good News*. That is because Jesus came on earth to bring us the Good News of God's love for us. Jesus told the Good News in stories. His stories were all about life in Palestine, the country in which he lived. We are going to read some of them in this book.

One of these Gospels was written by a doctor. His name was Luke. He was not one of the Jews, the people of Jesus. He was a Greek and his home was in faraway Greece. He had never met Jesus himself. His friend Paul had told him about Jesus, and Luke had come to believe in him. When Luke visited Palestine, he went about talking to people who had met Jesus and who had heard his stories. Luke collected stories that Jesus had told and wrote them down in his Gospel.

Doctor Luke liked, best of all, the stories Jesus had told about God's love for everyone – for Greeks as well as for Jews. Three of these stories were about things that had been lost, so Luke wrote them down together in his book. We are going to begin with these three stories, and we shall see how each one had a happy ending. We will start with the story Jesus told about a lost sheep.

The Lost Sheep

A man named Reuben lived in one of the little villages which nestled among the hills of Galilee, in the land of Palestine. He had his own little whitewashed house where he lived with his wife and children. Reuben worked hard on his piece of ground to grow food for his family. He grew barley for his wife to make bread, and vegetables for the stew-pot. He looked after his vines, so that there would be juicy grapes to make wine to drink – for water was scarce and precious. Figs for breakfast came from his fig-tree, and milk from his goats. The fruit from Reuben's olive-tree made olive-oil that was used for many things.

Reuben also had a flock of sheep. He had been a shepherd boy when he was young, and he knew all about shepherding. He loved having sheep of his own. He had started with only a few, but new lambs had been born every year, and now he had a hundred sheep in his flock. They grazed on the hills where they could find plenty of pasture, for Galilee had streams and rivers which made good, rich earth and lush, green grass.

Reuben's sheep grew fat on the fine pasture. But it was only on very special occasions that a sheep was killed to make meat. Sheep were kept for their milk and, above all, for their wool. When the fleecy wool had grown too long on the sheep's back it was cut and cleaned. His wife spun the wool on her spindle and then made cloth with it on her loom.

With the cloth she made fine, warm clothes for the whole family. Reuben and the children wore tunics and cloaks that she had made with the wool from the sheep.

Reuben always enjoyed being with the sheep. But he was too busy, now, to look after them himself. That was a job for his children. They liked looking after the sheep, for they were old friends. The family kept the same sheep for a long time and, like their father, Reuben, the children knew every single sheep in the flock. The little lambs were their greatest favourites, of course. They were often brought into the home to sleep at night, and they were the children's pets. The sheep, too, knew everyone in the family. They knew that Reuben and his wife and children looked after them.

Now it happened, one night, that one of the sheep was missing. Reuben's son had been out with them on the hills all day. Towards evening he led them to the fold where they would be safe for the night. As they went into the fold he counted them, one by one, as he always did. There were only ninety-nine sheep. One of them must have strayed from the flock during the day, and wandered off on its own. Now it was lost and in great danger.

Reuben's son ran back to the village as fast as he could, and burst into the house. 'Father!' he cried, 'one of the sheep is missing! It's one of the lambs, too!'

Reuben hurried to fetch his old shepherd's tools. He took them all, for he did not know what he might need. He tied his sling to his belt. It was a strip of leather, with a wide part in the middle which was hollowed out to hold a stone. A shepherd could find a pebble anywhere to put in his sling. Then he spun it round and round so that, when he suddenly let one end go, the stone shot out. An old shepherd like Reuben could shoot so cleverly with his sling that he could drop a stone exactly where he wanted. Reuben had learnt to use the sling when he was a boy, and he had taught his own sons too, of course. It might not be much use in the dark, unless the moon was full. But it was best to take everything, just in case.

Next Reuben tucked his horn into his belt. It was the horn of an animal, with a stopper in the open end to make a simple kind of bottle. Inside the horn was soothing oil, to put on cuts and bruises. Sheep often got scratched by sharp thorns. Sometimes they were wounded by wild animals. A shepherd never went out with the flock without his horn of oil.

Then Reuben picked up his rod. It was a club, made from the tough root of a tree, with bits of metal driven into it. It was a fine weapon for hitting out at wild animals trying to seize a sheep. It had a strap on the handle so that Reuben could tie it to his wrist. Now it hung close to his hand, ready for instant use.

With his other hand, Reuben picked up his staff. It was a strong length of wood taken from the branch of a tree. It was about as tall as a man. Every traveller carried a staff in his hand. He never knew when he might need it to defend himself against robbers or wild dogs. The shepherd needed it even more. His staff had a curve at one end. He could tuck the curved end under a sheep to lift it up, if he could not reach it with his hands. A shepherd's staff, with its curved end, is called his *crook*. Now Reuben had his crook, as well as his sling and horn and rod. He was ready to set out to search for his lost sheep.

It was quite dark by the time Reuben hurried off from the village, up into the hills. His son had told him where he had taken the sheep during the day. Reuben climbed the hillside with only one thought in his mind – he must find his precious lamb.

Reuben did not think about himself. When he was a boy, he was taught to be a good shepherd. The good shepherd cared for his sheep, not for himself. His life was hard. He had to be with his flock all the time – caring for them, finding pasture and water for them, and guarding them from danger. During the day it became terribly hot, and during the night it was often bitterly cold. Reuben wrapped his thick, woollen cloak about him and strode on. He was used to the dark and the cold and the dangers of the night.

There was just enough light from the moon to help him on his way. He walked quickly, for he had a long way to go. Besides, he must find his helpless lamb before some wild beast came across it. But, although he was hurrying, he was careful and alert. He knew well all the dangers of the night, up in the hills. Now that he was high up, the path was narrow. If he missed his foothold, he could easily fall over a steep precipice to his death. Beasts of prey might be lurking behind the bushes, crouching to pounce out on him. There were snakes in the undergrowth whose poison could kill. And there were sharp, cruel thorns on the bushes that he passed.

But Reuben was not afraid. He was ready for any trouble, with his staff in one hand and his rod clasped firmly in the other. He went carefully, but he did not slacken his pace. He was thinking all the time about his little lamb. He was listening intently for the tiny bleat that would tell him that it was alive and near.

On and on Reuben went, through the darkness and loneliness of the night. Sometimes he heard rustling in the bushes, and the noises of the night animals on the prowl. But most of the time all he could hear was his own footsteps in the still and silent night.

Then, at last, Reuben heard the sound he had been longing for. Away in the distance his sharp ear picked out the tiny bleat of a lamb. Eagerly he hurried towards it, till at last he could hear it close to him. But he stood near the edge of a precipice, and the bleating came from below him, over the edge.

Reuben lay down on the ground and crawled towards the edge of the precipice, till he could see over it. There, on the ledge below him, he could see his precious lamb. It was caught in a bush that had saved it from falling to its death on the rocks far below. Its whiteness stood out, in the moonlight, against the dark bush. There it was trapped, bleating helplessly.

Reuben murmured soft and comforting words to the lamb as he reached for his crook. He lowered it slowly and carefully over the edge and down into the bush. First he had to push away the branches which held the lamb fast, without hurting it. Now Reuben gently placed the curve of his crook under the lamb. He lifted it up towards him, inch by inch, till at last he could clasp it to him. Then, holding the trembling lamb close to his chest, he slowly moved his body back from the edge. Now both of them were safe, and Reuben sat up and fondled the lamb in his arms. It was shivering with cold and fear as it nestled against him and nuzzled his face. How glad it must have been to feel the warmth and the comfort of the master it knew so well!

Before he set off for home, Reuben tenderly felt all over the little lamb. There were bits of twigs and thorns to be pulled out, and scratches to be soothed from his horn of oil. Then they were ready for the return home. Reuben tucked the lamb inside his cloak, close to his chest, where it would be warm and safe. It was not long before it was asleep.

How happy Reuben was as he retraced his steps over the hills! Of course it had been a hard and dangerous journey through the night. But what did that matter? He had found his lamb, and his heart was full of joy. He was glad that ninety-nine of his sheep were safe in the fold. But he was much more glad that he had found the one which had been lost.

Reuben was so excited that he sang aloud as he came down the hillside towards the village below. The lamb was awake by now and he had put it across his shoulder. It was far into the night by the time he reached the village, but he did not care about that. Nor did the other villagers. Everyone had heard by now that Reuben had lost one of his sheep, and had gone off into the hills to search for it. His friends and neighbours were anxious for news of him. After all, Reuben had faced great dangers. They could not rest while he was out in the night.

The villagers were delighted to hear Reuben's merry voice in the distance. They rushed to unbar their doors and flocked out to greet him. 'I've found it! I've found my lamb!' Reuben was shouting. 'Come to my house! Come and share my joy!'

What a happy party they had that night! Reuben had to tell them all about his journey. The villagers would not be content until Reuben had told them how he had found his lamb. His wife hurried to get food and wine for her unexpected guests. They used up every scrap of food and every drop of wine in the house.

It was a long time before the village forgot the night when Reuben found his precious lamb. Of course, it was Reuben himself who made it so happy. He was so full of joy that everyone else simply had to share it. And while everyone was making merry, Reuben's wife was thinking to herself: 'What a good man Reuben is! Why, he is more full of joy over finding that one lost lamb than over all the other ninety-nine who were safe in the fold!'

When Jesus had ended his story, he said: 'It is just like that with God. He is your heavenly Father. He loves every one of his children, just as Reuben loved every one of his sheep. He knows each of you, he loves each of you, he cares for each of you. You are his sheep. He cannot rest if one of you is lost to him. And how happy he is when he finds you again!'

The Lost Coin

Stories Jesus told were always interesting and people loved to listen to them. That was because his stories were about ordinary, everyday things. Sometimes he made them up. Sometimes they were about things that had really happened. But every story told about God.

The stories of Jesus were never forgotten. Those who had heard them told them to other people. That was how Doctor Luke heard them when he came to the land of Jesus.

Jesus grew up in the hill-country called *Galilee*. People lived there in small towns and villages. In the villages, men worked as farmers and fishermen and shepherds. In the towns, men worked as carpenters and potters and weavers. In both villages and towns, mothers looked after their homes and children. This story is about a mother who lost something very precious in her home.

Mother Rachel lived in a small town in the hill-country of Galilee. She and her husband had four children – three boys and a girl. Her husband was a good man, honest and hardworking. He was a carpenter, and every morning he went off early to work at his trade. His eldest son went with him, for he was learning to be a carpenter, just like his father. The two younger boys went off to school. That left just Mother and her little daughter, Ruth, at home.

There was one day in the week when the whole family was together. That was God's day, just like our Sunday. It was called the *Sabbath*. No work was done on the sabbath day. The whole family went to church to worship God. They spent the rest of the day happily at home.

Our story happened on an ordinary weekday, when only Mother Rachel and her daughter Ruth were at home. That morning the family got up at daybreak, just the same as usual. Everyone had a job to do, and there was the usual rush to dress and wash and have some breakfast. They ate some fruit – figs and olives and raisins. They drank the milk from the family goat. Then the two younger boys hurried off to school. The eldest boy helped his father to load up the donkey with their tools and with wood for the job they were doing that day.

Carpenters were very important because they built houses. First, they made a framework of wood so that the house would be square and strong. Then they laid beams across the top for the roof. The walls of the house were made of baked bricks of clay and straw. The stairs were outside the house. They led up to the flat roof where people spent much of the day. It was made of branches, laid across the beams, and covered with clay mixed with stones. Of course, the roof had to have a low wall around it so that no one could fall off.

Carpenters made many other things, too. They made doors and chests and ladders and stools for the home. They made yokes and ploughs for the farmer, and wheels for the potter. They were always busy and they worked hard. But they did not earn a lot of money. Mother Rachel had to watch every penny so that she could feed and clothe her family. But she did not mind because they were such a happy family. Besides, they had good neighbours and plenty of friends.

She spent her money wisely and well. But she knew that, if her husband fell ill and could not work, she would be able to buy food with the family treasure, the money that had been given to her on her wedding day. You would never believe where Mother Rachel kept the precious coins. They were not put in a bank. They were not locked up in a chest. They were not hidden in a hole in the ground. The coins had been strung together like a necklace. Mother Rachel wore the chain of coins around her head. It covered her long white veil and kept it in place.

This chain of coins was the most valuable thing that Mother Rachel possessed. Every Jewish girl proudly wore her wedding gift around her forehead, after she was married. It showed that she was a married woman. It was her finest piece of jewelry, too. It was precious because it had been her wedding gift. It was precious, too, because it was the family treasure. You can imagine how carefully Mother Rachel looked after her chain of coins.

The coins were quite small. They were called *drachmas*. They were really Greek coins, but the Jews used them as money in those days. Even then each coin was not worth a great deal, but to a poor carpenter's family it seemed a fortune. No wonder that it was the family treasure. No wonder that Mother Rachel guarded it so carefully.

On the morning of our story, Mother Rachel got on with her jobs just the same as usual. Little Ruth helped her, for girls did not go to school. They stayed at home learning how to care for the homes that they would have when they were grown up.

First of all, Mother Rachel tied back the long flowing sleeves of her dress, so that they would not get in the way. Then she began to clean and tidy the house. It would have seemed a strange house to us. There were no separate rooms – it was all one big room. Nor was there any 'upstairs'. For, you will remember, the stairs were outside the house and led up to the flat roof.

One part of the big room was raised up, like a platform. That was where the family lived. They slept on the platform and had their meals there, too. The rest of the room was just a floor of bare earth. That was where the animals were kept, for they were brought indoors at night. They were tied to the manger where their food was kept. If a mother had a little baby, she laid it on clean straw in the manger, during the day. It would be safe and snug and warm there, while she got on with her work.

The floor of bare earth was always covered with a thick layer of dust. There was a lot of straw there, too, for the animals. No mother could keep that part of the house clean. But, of course, Mother Rachel always kept the platform clean for the family. She swept it each day with her broom. It was simply a stick, with palm leaves tied to it. But it was impossible to sweep the bare earth where the animals stayed.

There was something else that was strange about a Jewish house, too. It was very dark. There was only one small window – sometimes none at all. That was so that thieves could not get in. There was only one door, and that was quite small, too. Father had to stoop down to pass through it. Now you can see why the house was so dark. But that did not matter, because the family spent most of the time out of doors and up on the flat roof. The house was to protect them from the heat of the day and the cold of the night.

This was why the lamp was so important. It was made of clay by the potter. It had to be looked after very carefully, and this was Ruth's job. While her mother was cleaning and tidying the house, Ruth cleaned the lamp. Then she filled it with olive-oil and put in it a new wick, made of flax. The lamp had to burn well all through the day and the night. Because of the darkness of the house it was kept alight the whole time.

When the jobs had been finished inside the house, Ruth and her mother went outside to make the daily bread. Ruth brought some barley from the big jar in which it was kept. The grain had to be pressed between two flat stones, called *mill-stones*, to make flour. It was hard work, turning the handle fixed to the heavy mill-stone, and Mother was glad to have Ruth helping her. The flour was collected on a cloth. When there was enough flour, Ruth helped her mother make it into dough. Then they cooked small, flat, round loaves on the clay oven. The loaves were stored away, ready for the evening meal. That was the chief meal of the day, when the whole family were together again.

When the main jobs were all done, Ruth was free to go and play with her friends until the boys came home from school. They played on the flat roofs of their homes and the houses were built so close together that they could step from one roof to the next. Ruth scampered up the outside stairs, up on to the roof. Then she ran across the flat roofs until she found where her friends were playing.

Mother Rachel went back into the house. She untied her sleeves, for she was going to the well to fetch water in her big water-jar. She looked forward to meeting the other women at the well each day, and chatting with her friends. Naturally she wanted to look her best. She tidied her dress and straightened the veil on her head. She felt for her chain of coins, to make sure that it was straight. But, as she felt it with her fingers, she had a dreadful shock. It felt just as if one of the coins was not there. Quickly she pulled the chain off her head. There was no doubt about it. She could see the empty space in the chain where one of the coins had dropped off. One of her precious coins was lost!

What a state Mother Rachel was in! First she rushed outside – perhaps it had dropped off while she had been turning the mill-stone. But it was not there, she could soon tell that. Then she ran back indoors. She seized the lamp and hurried up the steps on to the platform to look there. She was so anxious and worried that she was sobbing as she searched. She searched everywhere. She moved every piece of furniture to make sure that the coin was not underneath. She looked in every nook and cranny. But her lost coin was nowhere to be seen. It was not on the platform.

Now there was nothing else to do but search through the thick layer of dust and straw on the rest of the floor. She took her broom and began to sweep over it carefully. She perched the lamp wherever she could so that it would give her some light to see by. She went over the whole ground. She looked in the corners. She even emptied the manger. But her precious coin was nowhere to be seen.

Anyone else might have thought it hopeless to look for a small coin in all that layer of dirt. But Mother Rachel never even thought of giving up. 'It must be there somewhere,' she said to herself. 'I must search more carefully. I must find it.' Now she put her broom away. She took the lamp, and went down on her hands and knees. She started in the farthest corner of the earthen floor. She put the lamp on the ground beside her. She began going carefully over every inch of the earth. There was no other way. She would go on until she found it. She carefully took up each handful of dust and straw, sorting it piece by piece under the lamp.

Mother Rachel did not notice how the time passed. She did not notice how her back ached, and her knees grew sore, and her eyes smarted, and her mouth was choked with dust. She did not even notice when the boys came back from school, and ran off happily to play when they saw that she was busy. Inch by inch she moved across the ground as the minutes ticked by.

It was afternoon, now, but she had not got up from the dusty earth. She could think of nothing else except finding her lost coin. She would not stop until she found it. Now she had reached the other side of the room, the lamp beside her. Several times she had felt something hard in the dirt, and her heart had leapt with excitement. But each time she had been disappointed. Now, once more, her fingers felt something in the straw – small and round. She pulled it out and held it up to the lamp. There was no doubt this time. It was her lost coin, her precious coin!

Mother Rachel cried out in her joy, laughing and weeping with delight. She got up, as best she could, from her stiff knees, clutching her coin. She hurried to the door and cried out. Her friends and neighbours came quickly, wondering what could be wrong. But there was nothing wrong now. 'I've found it! I've found my lost coin!' Mother Rachel cried out. 'Come! Come and share in my happiness!'

The house was soon full. Mother Rachel told the whole story of how she had lost her coin, and of her long search for it. Her friends were all married women – they would have felt just the same if they had lost part of their treasure. They could share her joy. What a happy time they had! But Mother Rachel was the happiest of all. Why, she was happier over finding that one lost coin than over all the other coins that hung safely on her chain!

When Jesus had ended his story, he said: 'It is just like that with God. He is your heavenly Father. Everyone is precious to him – just as every coin on her chain was precious to Mother Rachel. You are his treasure. He cannot rest if one of you is lost to him. And how happy he is when he finds you again!'

The Lost Son

Doctor Luke heard a third story that Jesus had told about something that was lost. This time it was not a sheep or a coin. It was a son. The sheep had been lost because it was silly and wandered away. The coin was lost by accident. But the son was lost quite deliberately. He went away from his father on purpose.

This story of the lost son has become one of the most famous of all the stories Jesus told. We can understand why. Jesus taught us that God is our heavenly Father. In this story we can see exactly what he is like – for the father in this story is God. That is why Jesus did not have to add anything, at the end of the story, to explain it. But this story is about us, too. For we often go away from God on purpose – just like the son who was lost.

Father Levi was a happy man. He had worked hard all his life and now he owned a big farm. Besides his wealth, he had been blessed with two fine sons. He looked forward to seeing them married and settled down. Then he might be blessed with little grandchildren, too. He was very happy as he looked out over his cornfields, his sheep and his cattle, his orchards and vineyards.

But his happiness was not to last. His elder son was quite content. He worked hard every day in the fields. But his younger son was restless and bored. He was tired of the dull farm where there was no excitement and nothing ever happened. He longed to go to the big, bright cities where everything was exciting and gay and where he knew he would be happy. One day he made up his mind. He could not stand the dreary farm any more. He went to his father. 'Father,' he said, 'give me my share of your money. I want it now. I'm leaving home and going away.'

Father Levi was sad when he heard this. He knew that money would not bring happiness to young Simon. But he loved his son too much to force him to stay at home. Besides, Simon must live his own life and learn for himself. Father Levi was too loving and too wise to try to stop him.

Simon knew that one third of his father's wealth would come to him, sooner or later. He claimed it now, as the law said he could. Of course, the farm and the house would go to his elder brother. He was the most important. Well, Jude was welcome to it! He liked working on the farm, so let him get on with it. Younger sons had to make their way in the world. He would soon show the family how clever he was. What a success he would be, once he got his share of his father's wealth!

Father Levi sold some of his sheep and cattle and part of his land. He sold exactly one third of his estate, so that Simon would have all that would come to him by law. Then he gave Simon the bag of silver.

Simon could not wait to be off. He put on his best clothes and tucked the bag of silver safely inside his belt. He could hardly stop to say good-bye. Father Levi watched him as he strode off down the road, and disappeared into the distance. He felt sad at losing his son. Now he could only watch and wait and long for him to come back.

How happy young Simon was as he got farther and farther away from that dreary farm! Now he would begin to live. What fun and pleasure and excitement he would have!

Simon did not need to cross the seas to find exciting cities. On the other side of the River Jordan there were fine Greek towns. We can still see the ruins of them today. One of the finest was called Gerasa. What a wonderful city it was! Simon could scarcely believe his eyes when he first gazed on its glorious sights and it was not long before he was joining in the life of the bustling city.

Simon was sensible enough to leave his money with the bankers. He went to them each time he needed more. There were so many things to spend it on in the gay city. He went to the hippodrome to see the horse races. There were new plays each week at the theatre. At the stadium there were sports in which the wonderful Greek athletes competed. Simon lounged at the public baths each day with his new friends. And, of course, there were wonderful shops where Simon was always buying fine new clothes. The gay young Jew had plenty to spend, and his father's money brought him lots of friends. Life was one long round of parties and Simon loved the music and dancing, the feasting and drinking and merry-making.

Some of the finest buildings in the city were temples of the Greek gods. Simon had been brought up to worship the one true God of the Jews, and to live strictly by his laws. He had been taught that the Greek gods were nothing but heathen idols, and that the Greeks were pagans. How glad he was to get away from all that! Anyway, he could not see much wrong with the Greeks. Why, now that he wore Greek clothes and followed Greek customs, he felt just like one of them. He was much happier here than he had been among his own people. How dull the Jews were, with all their strict laws. This was the life for him!

Simon was going to the bankers more and more often. They began to warn him that his money was getting low, but he took no notice. He never earned a penny in the big city. He was just spending his father's hard-earned money. One day Simon went to the bankers for some more money. They had to tell him that there was none left.

31

At first Simon did not worry. He had looked after his friends and spent money on them for a long time. Now they would look after him. But he got a shock when he went to them. They turned him away. They wanted nothing more to do with him. Now that his money was gone, his friends were gone too. He sold all his fine new clothes and soon he had nothing left.

Simon was very miserable as he wandered through the city streets. He was not among his own people – there was no one he could turn to for help. He was a stranger in a strange land. He was all alone – without friends and without money.

So Simon left the fine city. He went out into the countryside. Perhaps one of the farmers would give him a job. After all, he could do a good day's work on the land, with all that he knew about farming. But no one would give him work. His clothes were in rags by now, and he was starving. Then, at last, a farmer took pity on him. He said that Simon could look after his pigs. To be a swine-herd was the lowest job of all, but Simon was too hungry to be proud. The pigs were fed on the rough pods of the carob tree. They were like our runner-beans and tasted sweet. Simon was so hungry that he longed to stuff himself with the pigs' food.

The Greeks and the Romans kept lots of pigs. They liked eating pork, the meat from pigs, and they offered them as sacrifices to their idols. But the Jews hated the dirty animals that were offered to pagan gods. Their religion said that no Jew must have anything to do with pigs. Simon was, therefore, breaking the sacred law of his people, but he could not choose. He was a beggar. He had no home, no friends, no money. He was lost in a strange land.

Simon had plenty of time to think, as he guarded the pigs. 'What a fool I have been,' he thought to himself. 'I was much better off at home. I had everything I needed there. Look at me now. Why, even my father's servants are much better off than I am. I'll go back. Yes, I'll go back to my father. I'll own up to him that I have sinned against God. I'll tell him that I've been a bad son – not respecting my father and not honouring and obeying him. I've had my share of his estate, I know that. I can't expect him to take me back as his son. I'll ask him to let me be a labourer on his farm. I'll say to him: "I'm not fit to be treated like your son. Please take me on as a workman in the fields".'

It was a long, long journey back home. Mile after mile Simon hobbled along the dusty roads, eating any scraps he could find, sleeping by the roadside. No one would have recognized the dirty, tattered beggar as the proud son of Father Levi.

But there was one man who did. Father Levi had been sad and mournful ever since the day his young son had gone away. Every day he went up on the flat roof of his house. He sat there, looking into the distance, hoping and longing for his son to come back to him. It was Father Levi who recognized the tramp in rags and tatters, limping up the road. He hurried down the steps from the roof. He forgot all about his dignity and importance and ran down the road. He clasped Simon in his arms and hugged him tight, crying out in his joy.

Simon could hardly speak, as his father hugged and kissed him. Then he began to own up what a fool he had been. 'Father,' he said, 'I have sinned against God. I have been disrespectful and disobedient to you. I'm not fit to be taken back as your son. Just let me be one of your labourers.'

But Father Levi did not even listen. He was clapping his hands and calling for the servants. They came running out. 'My son has come back home,' he said. 'Fetch one of my finest robes for him, so that we may honour him. Bring one of my rings for his finger, so that he will have my authority. And don't forget a pair of slippers, too. We can't have him walking around barefoot, like a servant. Then you can kill the fatted calf and prepare a feast. We are going to eat and drink and be merry. My son was dead to me, and now he is alive again! He was lost, and now he is found!'

The servants hurried off to obey their master. Soon the whole household was bustling round and buzzing with the news. It was not often that they had a feast to look forward to, and the return of the young master was a happy time to celebrate. Everyone shared in Father Levi's joy.

What a feast they had! After all the eating and drinking came the merry-making. The flute-players made music for the round dance of the men. There was singing, stamping of feet, and clapping of hands. What a noise they made in their happiness! Anyone could have heard it a long way off.

Someone did. It was Jude, Simon's elder brother. He had spent a long, hard day in the fields and he was walking wearily back home. He heard the noise as he came near to the house. 'What's all that din for?' he called out to a servant. 'What are they all singing and dancing and shouting about?' The servant told him that Simon had come home and that the feast was in his honour. Jude was furious.

The servant ran in to tell Father Levi that Jude was back from the fields. 'Then ask Jude to come and take his place of honour at our feast,' said Father Levi.

'What!' shouted Jude at the servant when he came back. 'Does he think I'm going to rejoice, just because that good-for-nothing son of his has come back? Does he imagine I'm going to make merry to honour that lazy young rascal? I'm not going in there, and you can go and tell him so!'

The servant told his master what Jude had said. Then Father Levi went out himself to his elder son. He spoke kind and loving words to Jude. But Jude was too furious to listen. He was too angry even to be polite to his father, let alone speak to him respectfully as he ought. He was too rude even to let his father plead with him. 'All these years I've slaved on your farm!' he shouted at his father. 'I've always obeyed you! I've always served you! Did you ever give me a feast, so that I could make merry with my friends? No! But what happens when that wastrel of a son of yours comes back? Nothing's too good for him! All he's done is to throw away your money, enjoying himself in the big city. But he gets the fatted calf and a grand feast!'

Father Levi loved Jude just as much as he loved Simon. He could understand how Jude felt, and why he was so angry. He did not speak sternly to him. He did not complain of his lack of love. He simply put his arm around Jude's shoulder. 'Jude, my son, my dear son,' he said. 'You are always here with me. I know that I can rely on you. All that I have belongs to you, now that Simon has had his share. He is my son, just as you are. I love you both, dearly. It was only right to welcome him back home again. It makes me so happy to have him with me – just as it makes me happy to have you with me. You see, it is just as if he had come back from the dead. I was afraid I would never see him again, when he went away. He was dead – now he is alive again. He was lost – now he has been found. Come in with me, dear Jude. Come in and share my joy. Then my happiness will be complete.'

No wonder that fine story of the lost son became so popular. Our heavenly Father is just like the father in the story. He loves each one of us, just as Father Levi loved each of his sons. And we, like Jude, have to learn to love each other – just as the heavenly Father loves us.

The Friend Who Came at Midnight

This is another story from Doctor Luke's *Book of Good News*. It was a story Jesus told about prayer. Praying is talking to our heavenly Father. It is just like being with your earthly father. You like to be with him because you love him. You want to share things with him. Sometimes you have things to thank him for. Sometimes you want to own up to things you have done wrong. Sometimes you want to ask him for things.

This is a story about asking for things. Of course it would be greedy and selfish to be always asking for things. We might ask for things that were bad for us – or for things that we ought to work for. If we got everything we wanted just by asking we should be very spoiled children. Our father gives us what is good for us. He knows best.

It is just like that with the heavenly Father. He loves to give us good things because he loves us. It is right to ask for them. Jesus said that we should go on asking for them and he told this story to show just what he meant.

Father Simon lived in a small village that lay among the hills of Galilee. He was not rich or important. He worked on the land for hard-earned wages. But he was a happy man because he had his own little house in the village where he lived with his wife and children. He loved them dearly and he looked after them well. The Jews loved big families. They believed that children were given by God. Happy was the man who had been blessed by God with lots of children.

Father Simon's house was just like the house of Mother Rachel, who lost her precious coin. Father Simon's house was also made of wood and clay, and whitewashed with lime. The stairs were outside the house, and led up to the flat roof. Inside, it was all one big room, with a platform at one end for the family. The rest of the floor was simply earth, covered with straw for the animals. Every house in the village was just the same.

Our story happened at night-time, so we must see how Father Simon and his family went to bed. The Jews did not have clocks like we do. In fact, they did not bother much about the exact time. They lived simply by the sun. They went to bed soon after it was dark, and they got up soon after the sun rose. They divided the night into four parts, not into separate hours. They went to bed in the *evening*. That was between about six o'clock and nine o'clock. From about nine o'clock to twelve o'clock they called *midnight*. Then came the three hours called *cockcrow* and, at about three o'clock in the morning, began the three hours called *dawn*.

Every family would be settled in bed and asleep by the time the three hours called midnight began – that is, by about nine o'clock. The Jews believed that sleep was another gift from God. It would be sinful to lie awake! Rich men slept as the Romans did. They had fine beds, just like ours, made of wood and covered with cushions and blankets. But poor people, like Father Simon and the other village folk, slept on the floor on the platform. They lay simply on mats, or on mattresses filled with straw. During the day these mattresses were rolled up and put away in a corner, or in an alcove in the wall. When it was time to go to bed, the mattresses were brought out and spread on the platform. Some of these mattress beds were made big enough for two or three people to sleep on. Usually the children slept together like that.

On the night of our story, Father Simon and his family went to bed as usual. First he got the animals indoors and settled down. Then he bolted the door. This was done with a strong bar of wood. It went right across the door, and it was fixed on either side in two sockets on the door-posts. Now no one could get in through the door until he took the bar away. Next, all the beds were spread out on the platform. Then Father Simon and his wife and children settled down on their mattresses wrapped in their warm cloaks. The oil lamp gave a small, flickering light. Soon everyone was fast asleep and all was quiet and still.

A few houses away from Father Simon lived his friend Joses. Joses had a house just like Father Simon's. He had a family too, and they had all gone to bed at the usual time. Then, suddenly, when all was quiet and still, there came a loud banging at the door. Father Joses woke up with a start. Who on earth could it be at that hour of the night? There must be something wrong. No one ever disturbed the peace of the night in the little village.

'Who is there?' Joses called out. 'What do you want?'

'It is your friend Philip,' came the answer. 'I am on a journey, and I need food and shelter for the night.'

What a surprise it was for Father Joses! His good friend Philip! Why, he hadn't seen him for over a year.

'I'm coming, Philip,' he cried, leaping up from his bed.

Of course he had to move all the mattress beds and wake everyone up. Then he had to disturb the animals to get to the door and take down the bar that locked it. But nothing mattered compared with welcoming his friend into his home. Soon he had the door open and was embracing his dear friend, and kissing him on both cheeks as the custom was.

What a lot they would have to talk about over food and drink! His wife was soon bustling round to get a meal ready for the visitor.

Now there was another reason why Father Joses welcomed his friend so warmly into his house. Of course he was delighted to see Philip, even if it was night-time and the whole family had to be awakened. Philip had been very sensible. He had rested during the fierce heat of the sun. Now he had reached the village by the light of the moon.

But there were many dangers for a traveller, especially if he was all alone. Food and drink were very important in a hot country. A man could die of thirst in the heat. Shelter from the bitter cold of night was important, too. Besides this, there were no proper roads in the hill-country. There were robbers who hid behind rocks and pounced out on the lonely traveller. There were wild animals, too. You can see why the Jews never went on a journey unless they had to – and why they seldom went alone. Of course, they looked forward to going as pilgrims to the Holy City of Jerusalem. But then they all went together in one big merry group which they called a *caravan*.

You can see, too, why it was a sacred duty to welcome visitors and to give them food and shelter. A man could easily die if he were turned away. It would be a sin against God not to give hospitality to a visitor. It would have been a terrible thing for Father Joses not to have offered food and shelter to a needy traveller, whoever he was.

Joses helped Philip wash his hands and his face and his dusty feet. Then they sat down, ready to eat and drink and talk. But a terrible thing happened. Father Joses's wife came hurrying to him. 'There is not a scrap of bread in the house,' she said. 'We finished it all at supper.'

Father Joses was horrified. They could not make a meal without bread. No food for his hungry visitor – this was terrible! If he did not give Philip a meal he would not just be rude and unkind. He would be breaking the sacred law of his people. What on earth could he do?

There were no bread shops in the village in those days. There was only one thing for Father Joses to do. He must go and borrow some bread from his friend Simon. He would have some left.

Father Joses was not cross with his wife. Like every housewife, she baked the family bread every day. That was because bread goes bad very quickly in a hot country. Usually there was a little left over. But it was not her fault that none was left today. After all, it might only have gone bad and been wasted. She was sensible not to bake too much.

Father Joses got up quickly and asked Philip to excuse him for a moment. He wrapped his cloak about him as he went out. It was very strange to be out in the middle of the night. But there was plenty of moonlight, and it was only a few steps to Simon's house. He did not even stop to think how Simon would feel. There was only one thought in his mind – 'I must get bread for Philip.'

By this time, Father Simon and his family were all fast asleep, spread out on their mattresses. Their house was quiet and still. Then, suddenly, came the loud banging on the door. Father Simon was startled out of a deep sleep. What on earth was that terrible noise? Someone banging on his door? Whoever could it be at that time of night? Perhaps if he kept quiet it would stop and whoever it was would go away. Besides, if he called out he would start waking up the family. He muffled his cloak around his ears.

But it was no use. The banging went on. Now someone was calling his name. 'Simon! Simon! Wake up!'

Father Simon sat up, crossly. 'Who is it, making all that commotion at this time of night?' he called.

'It's your friend, Joses!'

'What on earth do you want?'

'I have a visitor. It's my old friend, Philip. He has been on the road all day. He needs food and shelter!'

'Then give it to him. He's your visitor, not mine.'

'But I can't!' Joses cried. 'We have no bread left in the house. Please lend me some!'

'I can't wake everyone up, just to please you,' Simon called, hoping that Joses would go away and leave him in peace. But Joses still went on banging at the door.

'I must have bread!' he shouted. 'Three small loaves – that's all I ask. We'll pay you back tomorrow!'

Unfortunately, Simon remembered that there had been some loaves left over from supper, so he could not tell Joses a lie and say that he had no bread. But he certainly didn't want to get up at that time of night. He was not just thinking of himself. He would have to wake up the whole family to get the bread, as well as disturbing the animals. Of course, Joses was his friend. But really this was too much to ask.

But Joses would not give up. He had no shame at all. He went on banging at the door as if it was the middle of the day, not the middle of the night. He just would not stop, banging the door and crying out for the loan of some bread. He would not go away until he got what he needed.

Father Simon could not be bothered to get up, just because Joses was his friend. It was his persistence that made Simon give in, in the end. He went on and on, banging and shouting. Then Father Simon saw that it was no good trying to get rid of Joses. He would not go till he got his bread. Simon got up from his mattress and fetched three of the loaves left over from supper. He had to move all the children's mattresses out of the way, waking them all up. He had to disturb all the animals to get to the door. He had to take the bar off the door to open it. Then he thrust the three loaves into the hands of his friend.

Joses was full of gratitude. He thanked Simon warmly for his great kindness. But Simon did not want to stay talking at that time of night.

He was only thinking of getting the door bolted safely and everyone settled down again. As for Joses, he hurried back to his house, clutching the loaves. He had got what he wanted by persisting – by keeping on asking. Now he had food for his friend Philip. Now he would be able to keep the sacred law and give food and shelter to the needy traveller.

When Jesus had ended his story, he said to the crowd of people listening to him: 'Many of you are fathers. Suppose your son wanted fish to eat. You would not give him a snake, would you? And if he wanted bread, you would not give him a stone. You are good to your children, even though there is evil in you. Your heavenly Father is perfectly good. Just think, then, what good things he will give to his children when they ask him!'

Now we can see that this fine story of Jesus was about asking God for things. It told how a man got what he needed simply by going on asking. But Jesus did not mean that God is just like grumpy Father Simon. Simon did not like being awakened in the middle of the night. But Jesus said that God always loves to listen to his children, whenever they call on him – day or night. He loves to give us his good things when we ask for them. Of course, he will not spoil us. Nor will he let us be greedy and selfish. In fact, it will be just the opposite. God's good things save us from being selfish and greedy. For the greatest gift of God is love.

Workers in the Vineyard

Stories Jesus told are found in the four Gospels in the Bible. All the stories we have read so far come from the Gospel written by Doctor Luke. Now we will read some stories from the Gospel named after Matthew, one of the twelve apostles of Jesus.

You will know by now what the Good News was. Jesus came to tell it. He spoke about it in his stories. He showed it, most of all, by the way he lived and the way he died. For the Good News was that God loves us. Jesus showed God's love to everyone. And many of his stories were about God's love and kindness and goodness to all his children.

Now, some people think they can bargain with God. They think: 'If I am very good God will have to reward me.' Peter, one of the apostles, was like that. One day he asked Jesus a question. 'Master,' he said, 'we have given up everything to follow you – our homes, our families, our friends, our work, everything. What reward will God give us for all that? How will he repay our goodness?' Jesus answered Peter by telling him this story.

Farmer Boaz was a rich man. He owned a big farm in the land of Galilee. He lived in a splendid house on his farm, and he had lots of servants. His chief servant was called his *steward*. The steward was a very important man. He had to look after all the other servants and arrange their work. Some of them worked in the house; others worked in the fields, where Farmer Boaz grew his crops. But the finest part of the farm was the vineyard.

Farmer Boaz had chosen a hillside for his vineyard, when he had planted it years before. He had worked hard to make his vineyard. Now it gave a wonderful harvest of grapes year by year. First, he had dug all over the ground with a mattock, a kind of pickaxe. When he had cleared all the stones from it, so that it was fine, rich soil, he had made terraces all down the slope of the hillside. On each of the terraces he had planted good vines so that he would get fine, juicy grapes.

Farmer Boaz had to protect his vines from animals and thieves, who came after the juicy grapes as harvest-time drew near, so he had made a wall of stones all round his vineyard. Then he had built a tall watch-tower in the middle of it. It was also made of stones and it was over ten feet high. A guard sat on top of the watch-tower, day and night. He could see over the whole vineyard from there and he was on the look-out for animals or thieves climbing over the wall. Branches were tied to posts around the top of the watch-tower. They sheltered the guard from the hot sun during the day and from the dew of night.

Foxes and jackals came after the grapes. They could easily get at them because the vines trailed along the ground, only propped up by short pieces of wood. That was why Farmer Boaz had made a jackal-scare, as it was called. This was just a pile of stones, whitewashed with lime. But it helped to scare away the jackals. Sometimes the vines were planted among fruit trees. They trailed from tree to tree, up among the branches. Animals could not reach them there, but thieves could. Now you can see why Farmer Boaz kept his vineyard guarded night and day when the grapes were getting ripe.

Grape harvest came in August or September, just before the rainy season began. All the grapes became ripe at about the same time, and they all had to be gathered in quickly before the heavy rains came. Farmer Boaz needed a great many workers to pick the grapes, so he went into the town, when grape-harvest came, to hire men from those who waited in the market-place for any work that was to be had.

It happened, one year, that Farmer Boaz had the finest harvest of grapes he had ever known. The vines were weighed down to the ground by the great bunches of fat, juicy grapes. His servants kept guard over the vineyard while the grapes ripened. Then came the day when they were ready for harvesting.

Farmer Boaz and his steward were up as soon as the sun rose. The steward was in charge of the work. Farmer Boaz went straight to the market-place to hire men. The best workers were there, waiting to be hired. They were good workmen, and they were ready to bargain for the best wage they could get for the day's work. They knew that the farmers needed plenty of workers for grape-harvest. Besides, times were hard. Many men could get no work at all, much of the year. They had to make as much money as they could while there was work.

The day's work began at six o'clock in the morning. It went on until six o'clock in the evening. The men waiting in the market-place at dawn were keen workers. They were ready to work all day, right through the heat of the sun. They should get a good wage for such hard and long work.

Now Farmer Boaz was a good man, fair and just. He did not try to be mean and to get workers for as little money as possible. He said to the men in the market-place: 'I will give you a denarius for a full day's work.'

A *denarius* was a silver coin of the Romans. The Jews did not like making coins of their own. That was because one of the Ten Commandments said that they must not make 'graven images'. They used Greek coins – like the drachmas that Mother Rachel wore on a chain round her forehead, you will remember. They used Roman coins, too, and the silver denarius was the most common money in their land. It was a fine day's pay for a labourer. Farmer Boaz had made a very generous offer to the men in the market-place.

The men talked among themselves. They soon decided. No other farmer would offer them such a fine wage. Their leader said to Farmer Boaz, 'We agree. We will work all day in your vineyard for a denarius.'

'Then hurry into my vineyard,' said Farmer Boaz. 'My steward is in charge. You will find him there. Tell him I have hired you.'

The men set off for the vineyard at once. Farmer Boaz was pleased. The harvesting of his grapes would get off to a good start, and he was soon back in the vineyard himself to see how the work was going. All the hired men were working hard, gathering the fat bunches of grapes in big baskets. But time was short, if all the grapes were to be safely gathered in. He went back to the market-place again before nine o'clock, looking for more men. He found some there and hired them at once.

'Go and work in my vineyard,' he said. 'You can trust me to give you a fair wage.'

Later in the morning Farmer Boaz went into the vineyard again. His steward hurried up to him. 'The men are all working well,' he said, 'but we shall never get the grapes picked in time at this rate. We simply must have more men, master.'

Again Farmer Boaz went back to the market-place. It was nearly midday, but there were still men there waiting for work. 'Hurry into my vineyard,' he said. 'We need more workers. You can trust me to give you a fair wage.'

It went on like that all day. Farmer Boaz had to hire more men again in the afternoon. They also trusted him to pay them fairly. By now the vineyard was buzzing with busy workers, gathering grapes as fast as they could. But there were still a lot more bunches to be picked. It was almost five o'clock now. There was only an hour left for work before sundown. But Farmer Boaz went again to the market-place, for every minute mattered. He was surprised to find some men lolling there.

'Why do you lounge around here all day, doing nothing?' he asked.

'We can't get any work,' one of them said. 'No one will hire us.'

That was quite true. The times were bad, and even good workers were often out of work. But these were men who were not very strong and could not work very hard. They seldom got any work at all. Farmer Boaz felt sorry for them. They, too, had wives and children to feed and to clothe. They needed money even more than the good workers, for they earned so little.

'You hurry into my vineyard,' said Farmer Boaz. 'There is still an hour of daylight left for work. I'll pay you what is right.'

The men went off to the vineyard at once. They were very glad to have some work to do, even if it was only for an hour. Of course, they could hardly expect to get much pay just for that, but they knew that Farmer Boaz was a good man. They were quite content to rely simply on his generosity.

At six o'clock the long day's work ended. All the hired men lined up for their wages. Farmer Boaz came out from the house and gave his steward a bag of coins.

'Give one denarius to everyone,' he ordered. 'Start with those I hired at five o'clock. Next, pay those I hired during the afternoon, then those that I hired during the morning. Those who started at dawn and have worked all day are to be paid last of all.'

Farmer Boaz went back to his house, and the steward began paying the workers. He did just as he had been ordered. He started with those who had worked for only one hour. How delighted they were when each of them was given a shining silver denarius! Why, it was a full day's pay

– and a very good one at that! How grateful they were to Farmer Boaz for his generosity! They could talk of nothing else all the way home.

Next, the steward paid those who had been hired during the day. First, he paid those who had worked for four hours, then those who had worked for six hours, then those who had worked for nine hours. Each of them was given a denarius, too. How pleased they were! A full day's pay – and a good one at that! They had simply trusted Farmer Boaz. He had paid them much more than they deserved.

Now the men who had worked the whole day long had to wait till last. They rubbed their hands with glee as they watched all the other workers being paid. 'Why,' they said to each other, 'these men are all getting a full day's pay! They've only worked for part of the day – some of them for only an hour – and each of them gets a silver denarius! Farmer Boaz is certainly in a generous mood – just think what we'll get! Of course, we did bargain with him for a silver denarius. But we have worked the whole day through. We shall certainly get a lot more than that!'

Imagine their surprise when at last their turn came. Each of them got exactly what he had bargained for – one silver denarius. They were furious. They started shouting at the steward and shaking their fists towards the house. They got so worked up that, in the end, they rushed up to the house making a dreadful din.

Farmer Boaz came out. 'What do you want with me?' he said courteously.

The ringleader was too angry to be polite. 'We want a fair wage!' he shouted, rudely. 'We've slaved all day in your vineyard! We've sweated all through the heat of the sun! Twelve solid hours – and you give us the same pay as those lay-abouts who've only done one hour! D'you call that fair? We want our rights!'

All of the men shouted in a chorus: 'We want our rights!'

Farmer Boaz addressed the ringleader politely. 'My dear sir, you seem to think that I have cheated you. I have done you no wrong. Didn't you agree with me to do a day's work for one silver denarius? That is exactly what I have paid you. You kept your part of the agreement. I have kept mine. That was our bargain. What are you grumbling about? Because I paid all the other men the same as you? But that's my business, not yours. Can't I do what I like with my own money? Why should you complain, just because I choose to be generous? Are you full of envy, just because I was kind to the other workers? You have got exactly what you bargained for. Now take your wages and be off – all of you.'

What a strange story that was! It turned everything upside-down. No farmer could afford to pay out money like that. He would be penniless in no time. That's not the way to make money and to get on in business!

But Jesus knew that very well. He deliberately turned everything upside-down in his story. After all, there would have been no trouble at all if Farmer Boaz had not ordered his steward to pay the last men first, and the first men last of all. He had done that quite deliberately so that the men who had bargained with him would learn their lesson.

This was not a story about how to make money. It was a story about God and his love. God is like Farmer Boaz. He loves to be generous to his children. Those who bargain with him get only what they bargain for. Those who simply trust in him receive far more than they could ever deserve or expect. But those who expect nothing receive more than they could ever dream of.

That was the answer to Peter's question. It is foolish to think we can bargain with God. We can only trust in him, and rely on his goodness and generosity.

The Unforgiving Governor

Jesus told this story, like the last one, to answer a question that Peter had asked him. Peter and his brother, Andrew, were two of the twelve apostles of Jesus. They had been fishermen, on the Sea of Galilee, before they became followers of Jesus. They were both big, strong men from their hard life in the open air, but they were very different from each other. Peter was a bluff man, head-strong and hot-tempered. He spoke without thinking, and his tongue often ran away with him, but he was stout-hearted and full of love for Jesus.

Andrew, it seems, was quiet and thoughtful, much slower than Peter, but he was always sensible and helpful. Because Peter and Andrew were so different, they sometimes quarrelled. Andrew often annoyed Peter and easily made him cross. Then, when Andrew said he was sorry, Peter had to forgive him.

One day Peter asked Jesus about this. 'When my brother offends me I know that I must forgive him,' Peter said. 'But how often should I go on forgiving him? I know that our religion says that you must forgive someone three times. But what do you say, Master? Would seven times be enough?'

'No,' said Jesus. 'You must go on forgiving him – seventy times seven, if need be.'

Now that makes 490 times. But, of course, what Jesus meant was that we must go on and on forgiving others when they offend us and he told this story to explain why.

There was once a mighty Emperor. He lived in a wonderful palace in his great capital city, and he ruled from there. But, of course, he could not know what was happening in every corner of his vast empire. He had to choose trusty servants to help him govern, and he appointed Governors to rule over each part of his great kingdom.

It was the duty of each Governor to see that the people in his part of the kingdom were loyal to the Emperor. As the Emperor's representative he had to see that everyone obeyed the laws and kept the peace.

A Governor also had to see that the taxes were collected properly. It cost a huge amount of money to rule such a mighty empire. Everyone in it had to pay taxes to the Emperor. The Governor organized the collection of the taxes and then he had to see that the taxes were sent to the Emperor in his capital city.

Of course, every Governor had to be loyal to the Emperor himself. A Governor was a great man in the land he ruled over for the Emperor. He was important and rich and powerful. But he had to be loyal and faithful to the Emperor and to obey any commands that the Emperor sent to him. If he were not, then, of course, the Emperor would dismiss him and punish him, and might have him put to death. You can see why wise Governors made sure that they ruled well and were loyal to the Emperor.

Now it happened that, over the years, the Emperor grew rather lazy. For a long time he had left his Governors to rule over his empire. He had not bothered to make sure that they were ruling well and justly. So long as there was peace throughout the empire he had not cared. He had not even bothered to see that the taxes were being properly collected and sent to him in his capital city. He lived a life of ease and luxury in his splendid palace. He went on enjoying himself, and his Governors went on ruling for him. They were never bothered by the Emperor.

Then, suddenly, it happened. Every Governor received a royal command. They were all ordered to come to the capital city at once. The Emperor had decided to go through their accounts and to see that the taxes had been properly collected each year and sent to him. The royal treasury was getting short of money. Either something had gone wrong with the tax collecting, or the taxes were not enough. Something must be done quickly.

No Governor could refuse the royal command to come to the capital city. But there was one who dreaded coming and had been quaking in his shoes ever since the order arrived. He had been very foolish over the years. His power had gone to his head. He had bought himself a fine house and a lot of land. He lived like a lord, and so did his wife and children. But he had stolen the money to pay for all his glory. And he had stolen it from the Emperor.

Each year this Governor had collected all the taxes. But he had not sent all the money to the Emperor. He had kept some for himself. Each year he had grown more and more greedy. After all, he thought, the Emperor would never know. He never bothered about checking the taxes. So the Governor cheated the Emperor, and each year he cheated him more and more.

No wonder this Governor was terrified. Now he would be found out. The Emperor would be furious and punish him severely. He would lose all his power and wealth. The Emperor might have him flogged, or imprisoned for the rest of his life, or beheaded. He was terrified. Whatever could he do to save himself?

The awful day came. The Emperor sat on his throne in his royal palace. All his courtiers were gathered around him. All the Governors were brought before him. Court officials read out the tax payments from each Governor. Many of them were praised by the Emperor for their honesty and their loyalty. Then came the turn of the Governor who had been dishonest. He was in debt to the Emperor. Each year his tax payments had been less and less. Now his debt had reached the huge total of ten thousand talents!

Now a talent was not a coin but a certain weight of gold or silver. It was worth many thousands of coins. In fact, it was the largest sum of money that there was. Only very rich men ever even saw a talent. And the Governor owed ten thousand of them to the Emperor! That was the largest number that the Jews had in their counting. For his story, Jesus had deliberately chosen the most precious weight of money and the biggest number that the Jews knew. It made an enormous debt which no one could possibly repay.

Everyone in the royal court was shocked when they heard what the Governor owed to the Emperor. They waited to hear his punishment. It would certainly be a terrible one.

The Emperor was furious.

'You wicked scoundrel!' he cried. 'You have been cheating me for years! You owe me ten thousand talents! You can never repay your debt. But at least everything you possess will go towards it. You and your wife and your children will all be sold as slaves. Your house and your lands and everything you possess will be sold. That will punish you for your wickedness!'

The Governor shook with terror. There was only one thing he could do to save himself from that terrible fate. He threw himself on the floor and grovelled at the Emperor's feet, weeping and wailing.

'Have patience, Lord,' he wept. 'I will pay back everything I owe you.'

The Emperor knew very well that the Governor could never pay back his huge debt, but he felt sorry for him, grovelling there before his throne. His anger melted away and he was full of pity. He decided to forgive the Governor. He did not dismiss him. He did not condemn him for being so disloyal and dishonest. He did not even make the Governor promise to pay the taxes honestly in the future. He simply forgave the Governor his huge debt – every part of it. The Governor went out of the palace a free man – everything forgiven.

The Governor was still trembling as he walked down the palace steps and into the market-place. What a terrible moment that had been! To be sold into slavery – what a fate! But he had escaped it – that was the great thing. To throw himself on the Emperor's mercy had been the only thing to do. It had meant grovelling on the floor, of course, and he hated that. What a fool he must have looked, with the whole court and all the other Governors looking on! Fancy him, the mighty Governor, having to grovel like that!

The more he thought about it the more angry he became. His pride had been hurt and he could think of nothing else. He completely forgot the terrible fate he had escaped. He completely forgot that only the Emperor's kindness and forgiveness had saved him. He did not feel grateful. He felt angry for being humbled in front of everyone else.

Then, in the crowd, he suddenly caught sight of a man from the land he ruled over. He was a very poor man and he owed the Governor a small sum of money. 'Why, there's that fellow Demetrius!' the Governor said to himself. 'He owes me one hundred silver denarii. It's rascals like that, owing me money, that landed me before the Emperor! I'll teach him to make me grovel!'

The Governor rushed at the poor man. 'You wicked scoundrel!' he shouted, seizing the poor man by the collar. 'You owe me a hundred denarii! Pay your debts, you rascal!'

The Governor was quite within his rights. The law said that, if a man owed you money, you could seize him by the collar and demand it from him. If he could not pay it, you could have him sent to prison. He would have to stay there until he paid his debt.

The poor man shook with terror. A hundred denarii was a huge sum of money to a poor peasant. He could never repay it. He threw himself on the ground and grovelled at the Governor's feet, weeping and wailing.

'Have patience, Lord,' he wept. 'I will pay back every denarius I owe you!'

But the Governor had no pity on the poor man, grovelling at his feet. He showed him no mercy. He had him dragged off to prison. Let the rascal rot in a dungeon until he had paid back every one of the hundred denarii!

A crowd had quickly gathered in the market-place while this was going on. They had watched it all. They felt very sorry for the poor man, for he would spend the rest of his life in a dark and gloomy dungeon. The story of what had happened spread quickly. It was not long before it reached some of the courtiers. They were horrified when they heard what the Governor had done, and how he had treated the poor man who owed him a hundred denarii. Why, it was not long since they had seen the dishonest Governor grovelling before the Emperor. He had been forgiven a huge debt of ten thousand talents. Yet he could not forgive a poor man who owed him only a small sum!

They talked about it among themselves in the palace. It was not long before the story reached the Emperor's ears. At once he sent for the Governor.

'You wicked scoundrel!' the Emperor cried in his anger. 'I forgave you your huge debt when you pleaded with me. But you could not forgive that man his little debt when he pleaded with you. Very well! You have chosen your own punishment. I will treat you exactly as you treated him! I send you to prison, just as you sent him. You will be in the hands of the torturers, and you will stay there until you have repaid every penny of your debt. Take him away!'

It was no use grovelling and pleading now. The Governor had had his chance. Now he was sentenced to the fate that he had chosen. He was dragged away to spend the rest of his life in a dark and gloomy dungeon. The torturers would give him endless punishment, but he had brought it all upon himself.

That story was a fine answer to Peter's question. Jesus had told him that we must go on forgiving others without limit. Now we can understand why. It is simply because we are forgiven so much ourselves.

We are like the Governor in the story. We owe to God a huge debt that we can never repay. He gives us everything. He forgives us freely, when we ask him. The debts that others owe to us are small and tiny, compared with the huge debt we owe to God. Once we understand that, we learn to forgive others. But if we do not forgive others, we cannot expect God to forgive us. That is only right and fair.

Jesus ended his story by saying: 'That is how God will treat you, if you behave as the Governor did. He cannot forgive you, if you cannot forgive others. You must forgive each other endlessly, just as God forgives you endlessly. If you have a hard, unforgiving heart you shut yourself away from God.'

Now you can see why Jesus taught us to pray to God each day: 'Forgive us our trespasses, as we forgive those who trespass against us.'

A Rich Man and His Servants

Many of the stories Jesus told were about money. Times were hard in Galilee and it was not easy to earn a living. Some men could not find work. Others worked very hard for little pay. Jesus told his stories to people who were worried about keeping their homes going, and about getting food and clothes for their children. That is why worry about money comes into the stories.

Rich men had worries about money, too. Poor people worried about getting money. Rich people worried about keeping their money. The poor folk kept what little money they had at home. Married women, like Mother Rachel, you will remember, wore their treasure on a chain around their foreheads. Some wrapped their money up in a cloth, and hid it in a hole in the ground. Men wore jewelry, just like women. They wore rings on their fingers and rings in their ears. A man's ear-rings or finger-rings might be his treasure. He carried it around with him safely, too.

Rich men worried about thieves and robbers. They robbed travellers on the roads. They stole from houses by night. They even raided a rich man's house in broad daylight, if it was in a lonely place. That was why rich men kept their money in banks. Bankers were shrewd and clever men. They looked after money. They lent money out and became rich by charging interest on loans. They changed money, too, for people used coins from other lands. Some were Greek coins, like the drachmas of Mother Rachel. Some were Roman coins, like the silver denarius that Farmer Boaz gave to each of his workers. Some came from the land of the Phoenicians, too, for they were great traders. Whatever his money was, a rich man could be sure that the bankers would accept it.

Sometimes a rich man did not put all his money in the bank. This story is about a wealthy man who did something else with his money.

Lord Jabez came from a noble family and he was a very rich man. He lived in the city, where he had a fine town house and many servants. He owned farms in the country, and he rented them out. He got a lot of money from his rents, but most of his wealth came from his business. He was a shrewd merchant, buying and selling rich and precious things from other lands. Often he had to travel abroad on his business.

When Lord Jabez went to other lands he left his money safe with the bankers. They paid him interest on it, because they made even more money by lending some of it to others. But Lord Jabez was a very clever businessman. He thought of something else that he could do with his money, when he went abroad. It should bring him in more money than the interest the bankers paid.

One morning, the house of Lord Jabez was all hurry and bustle. He was going abroad on a business trip, and the servants were busy helping him prepare for his journey. Before he left, Lord Jabez sent for three of his servants. They were slaves whom he had owned for many years. That did not mean that they were cruelly treated. Slaves could be important men. They looked after their master's children, and some became teachers. They looked after their master's house and lands. Some even looked after their master's money and business affairs.

The three slaves were surprised when they came into the room. In front of Lord Jabez there were eight heavy money-bags. They were on the floor, for they were much too big and heavy for the table. There were five money-bags in one group, and two in another group. One money-bag stood all by itself.

'As you know, I am going abroad,' Lord Jabez said to them. 'I am not going to leave all my money with the bankers this time. I've decided to trust some of it to you three. See what you can earn for me with it. James – you have these five bags. There is one talent of silver in each bag. You're a clever and able man. Use your five talents well, and make as much money for me as you can. John – you have these two bags. You're sensible and honest. You should be able to make good use of two talents. Paul – here's one talent for you. I have not found you very helpful in the past, nor eager to please me. This is your chance to show what you can do. I shall be away a long time,' Lord Jabez ended. 'When I return, I shall want a full account from all three of you. Do your best. You can be sure that I shall reward you, if you serve me faithfully and loyally.'

Then he set off on his travels.

Lord Jabez had been very wise in the way he had shared his money among his three slaves. James was the cleverest by far. He was devoted to his master, too. He would make good use of five talents. John was not so clever, but he was reliable and solid and trustworthy. He would work hard to please his master. Paul was a surly man. He never did anything unless he had to. What he did with his one talent would be a real test for him.

Now, you will remember that a talent was the biggest sum of money in those days. It was a weight of silver or gold, the most precious metals. These were talents of silver. Each talent weighed about one hundred pounds.

James was delighted that his master had trusted him with so much money. Five talents – it was a huge sum! He had never seen so much money before. He began to think of all the things he could do with it to make more money for his master. Nothing pleased him more than winning praise from Lord Jabez.

James decided to go into big business. That was the best way to make a lot of money. He knew quite a bit about it from helping his master. He was too clever to risk his money in foolish ventures. He would trade shrewdly and carefully, just as his master did. He began by spending all his time in the market and down at the harbour. He studied the prices of everything, and found out what were the most profitable things to trade in. He was soon busy, buying and then selling.

Everyone needed to buy corn and barley for making bread, and oil for lighting and cooking. Oil was used for making perfumes, too. Perfumes were a luxury that only the rich could afford – James did well selling them. Then there was fish from the Sea of Galilee. It was salted, to keep it fresh, packed up in boxes, and then sent all over the country. It was also taken in ships to other lands. James put some of his money in the fish trade. He traded in dried fruits, too.

But James did not buy and sell only in the home market. He soon found that he could make a lot of money from buying luxuries and selling them to the rich people. They were brought from other lands in ships and by camels. There were costly scents and spices that came in camel-caravans from the East. James bought up the incense and pepper they carried and made a fine profit when he sold it in the market. He traded in silks and sandalwood from other lands. He bought bales of the fine cloth that came from Damascus and so was called 'damask'. He bought cloth from Phoenicia, dyed with rich and costly purple, that only kings and nobles and rich men could afford. That made a fine profit, too.

How busy James was! All day and every day he was hard at work with his master's money. Month by month his profits grew. By the time Lord Jabez returned, he had made five talents in clear profit. His five talents had grown into ten talents. He had doubled his master's money! He was delighted, and eagerly looked forward to telling his master what he had done for him.

John worked hard with his two talents, too. But he was much more cautious than James. He did not venture into foreign trade. But that was wise, for he did not understand it properly. He was much happier trading in the market-place with things that ordinary folk needed. He did not know enough about luxuries like perfumes and spices, silks and cloth and dyes. He was not going to risk losing any of his master's money. He might easily get cheated by the crafty and cunning merchants. He might pay too much for things and then have to sell them for less, and so lose money.

John set up his stall in the bazaar. Every morning, bright and early, he was down in the market-place. He was very cautious, buying things that he knew would sell. Then he took them to his stall and spent the whole day there, selling his goods. People soon got to know him. They soon found that he was an honest man, and never sold anything that was poor in quality. Of course, people loved to haggle with him over prices, as they always do in the East. They liked to argue and try to get things cheaper. But John knew the true value of his goods, and he made sure he got the price they deserved.

He sold corn and wine and oil in the bazaar. He sold fruits and fish, brought in by the local farmers and fishermen. Sometimes he bought the famous balm from Jericho, a kind of gum used for ointment. But mostly he bought things that came in from the countryside round about and sold them to the townsfolk.

John made his profits by sheer hard work. He was so careful that he never lost a penny of his master's money. His profits grew steadily, month by month. He put some of them in the bank, so as to get more money from interest. He invested some of his profits in good, sound businesses. He became one of the best-known traders in the town, and one of the most popular for his honesty.

By the time his master returned, John had made two talents in clear profit. His two talents had grown into four talents. He had doubled his master's money! How delighted he was. And how eagerly he looked forward to telling his master what he had done for him.

Paul was very different. He knew that Lord Jabez was a hard and shrewd businessman. He cleverly got other people to do the work and make money for him – and woe betide them if they lost any! No, he was not going to risk his master's wrath. He decided to keep his talent safe. He wrapped up the heavy money-bag in a cloth and buried it in a hole in the ground. It would be safe there until Lord Jabez returned. Then he could have his precious talent back again.

At last the day came when Lord Jabez returned from his long travels. The house was all hurry and bustle as the servants unpacked his belongings and prepared dinner for him. When he was seated at table, Lord Jabez sent for his three slaves to render their accounts.

James came in first, staggering under his heavy load of money-bags.

'You entrusted me with five talents, Lord. See, I have made five more talents. I have doubled your money!' James said, proudly.

'Well done!' said his master. 'What a faithful and trustworthy slave you are! You have been loyal to me in a few things. Now I will put you in charge of more important affairs. I give you your freedom, as a reward for your loyalty. Come, join me at table, now that you are a free man. Sit with me, and share in my feasting.'

John came in next, carrying four heavy bags. 'You entrusted me with two talents, Lord. See, I have made two more talents. I have doubled your money!' he said, proudly.

'Well done!' said his master. 'What a faithful and trustworthy slave you are! You have been loyal to me in a few things. Now I will put you in charge of more important affairs. I give you your freedom as a reward for your loyalty. Come, join me at table, now that you are a free man. Sit with me, and share in my feasting.'

Then Paul came in, carrying his one money-bag. He dumped it on the floor near his master. 'I knew what a hard man you are, Lord,' he said. 'You make money from the work of others, and collect what you have never earned. I was afraid to risk losing any of your money. I hid it in the ground and kept it safe for you. Here is your talent. I have not lost a penny of it.'

Lord Jabez was very angry with Paul. 'You lazy rascal!' he cried. 'So you knew I was a hard man, did you, making money from the work of others and collecting what I have never earned! Then you should have put my money with the bankers – at least I would have got interest on it! From you I get nothing at all!'

Then Lord Jabez turned to the slaves waiting on him. 'Take the talent from him,' he ordered. 'Give it to my friend here who had five talents and doubled them. And throw that useless wretch out into the night!'

It is from this fine story of Jesus that we get our word *talent*. A talent is any gift we may have. There are many different kinds of talents. You can have a talent for sport or music or art or study. You may have a talent for making things, for growing things, for creating things. Some are gifted with their hands, others with their bodies, others with their brains. Every one of us has some gift from God. It is a talent that he has entrusted to us.

God wants us to use our talents, and to do all that we can with them for him. Then we find that they grow. We must not be like Paul, and hide our talents away and refuse to use them. If we do that, we are cheating God. But, if we love our Lord, we shall use our talents wisely and well in his service. Nothing will please us more than to win his praise.

Bridesmaids at a Wedding

Stories Jesus told were always about the daily life of the people among whom he lived, in the hill-country of Galilee. That was why his stories were so interesting, for everyone could understand them. That was why he became such a popular teacher. For, in his stories, Jesus was teaching about God. His stories were about the Good News that he brought – of God's love for all his children.

Jesus had grown up in Galilee, in the little town of Nazareth. He came from a poor home. When he grew up, he worked as a builder with stone and wood. When he began God's work, he mixed with all kinds of people. Some were rich, some were poor. Some were good people, some were bad people. Some lived in towns, some in villages. Some worked on the land, some worked at crafts and trades. Jesus knew all about how people lived – in towns, in villages, in the countryside. He knew their joys and their sorrows. He shared in them.

The happiest times, of course, were parties and feasts and banquets. They did not happen often. They were for special, joyful occasions. The happiest times of all were weddings. Jesus knew all about weddings. There is one story in the Bible of how he went to a wedding. Naturally, some of his stories were about weddings, too.

The Jews had their own wedding customs. They were different from ours, as we shall see in this story Jesus told about a young couple who were married. We will call them Susanna and Levi.

A marriage was always important. It concerned both families, and it had to be carefully arranged. Susanna and Levi did not decide for themselves. It was their fathers who decided that they should marry each other. First of all, their fathers met together and talked it over. They decided that it would be a good match, and that Susanna and Levi should be married. Then they talked about money matters.

In early times a man bought his bride from her father. He paid money for her, or worked for her father for a certain time. Now there was a marriage settlement of money between the two fathers. Some of the money went to the bride's father. Some of it belonged to the bride herself. You will remember that Mother Rachel, like all married women, wore her marriage money in a chain around her forehead.

When the marriage had been agreed, the two families met together in Susanna's home. This was a very solemn time. Susanna and Levi were engaged to each other. This was called their *betrothal* – for they gave their 'troth' or 'true promise' to each other. Now they belonged to each other for always. Their betrothal was so sacred that it was just like being married. It lasted for one year, before they set up home together. If Levi had died during that year, Susanna would have been a widow all her life. But nothing so sad happened. Levi spent the year saving hard to buy a house. Susanna was getting all her clothes and the things she would need for her home.

At the end of the year's betrothal came the happy wedding. The celebrations went on for a whole week, for a wedding was the happiest time of all. This was why weddings were held in the autumn, after the harvest was gathered in. The fathers of both Susanna and Levi were farmers. Most of their friends worked on the land, too. All the crops had to be safely gathered and stored in the barns. Harvest was the busiest time of the whole year. Once it was over, everyone could take a holiday. There could be no finer holiday than a whole week of parties and jollity and merry-making in honour of Susanna and Levi. It began with the joyful wedding-feast. It was held in the evening at the house of the bridegroom. All the friends of the two families were invited to share in the banquet.

Everyone was bustling round in the house of Levi, that day of the wedding-feast. It was a big house, for his father was a well-to-do farmer. Many guests were coming and a rich banquet was being prepared for them. All day, Levi's mother and her women friends had been busy getting ready, and seeing that the servants arranged everything properly. Now it was getting dark and they had to hurry to have everything ready for the guests.

Levi had his best friends with him. They were called his *groomsmen*, since Levi was the bridegroom. They were his escort, looking after him and helping him to care for the guests. They were all dressed in their finest clothes. But they made sure that Levi was the smartest of all. They were like the 'best man', as he is called, at a wedding today. During the wedding week they were excused from their work and from all their duties. During the whole week their duty was to wait upon Levi, and to help him in every way that they could.

Susanna had her best friends with her, too. They were called her *bridesmaids*, just as they are today. Susanna had ten bridesmaids altogether. They were girls of her own age and she had chosen them to be her maids. One of their tasks, of course, was to help Susanna to prepare herself for her wedding. It was the greatest day in her life, and she had to look as pretty as she could. All the bridesmaids wore their finest dresses, covered with embroidery. But they made sure that Susanna was the prettiest of all.

Susanna and her ten bridesmaids had to be quite ready by the time evening came. They had to wait for Levi to come and fetch his bride. He would be escorted by his groomsmen. When they arrived, Susanna and her bridesmaids would go out and join them. Then Susanna and her bridesmaids and Levi and his groomsmen would all form a happy procession. They would make their way to the house of Levi for the grand wedding-feast.

As this wedding procession took place in the evening, it was dark and lights were needed to show the way. It was the duty of the bridesmaids to provide these lights. Sometimes they carried lights on top of poles. They were pieces of cloth, soaked in oil which burned in small copper holders, fixed to the tops of the poles. In India today weddings are still held in the evenings, and the people of India have these torchlight processions – just as Jews used to do.

But at the wedding of Susanna and Levi the bridesmaids carried lamps. They were quite small lamps that could be held by the handle in one hand. A lamp was made of clay. It had a hole at one end for pouring in olive-oil. In the other hole was a wick made of flax. A simple shade around the wick protected the flame from the evening breeze. Poor people could only afford one lamp in their peasant houses. But this was the wedding of farmers' children. Each of Susanna's ten bridesmaids carried her own lamp.

Now it was very important for the bridesmaids to light up the procession to the wedding-feast. It was a terrible disgrace for the bridesmaids not to have their lamps burning brightly, but this was exactly what happened at the wedding of Susanna and Levi.

Susanna and her bridesmaids were ready as soon as darkness fell. They had to be ready early, for they did not know when Levi and his groomsmen would arrive. As we have seen, the Jews never bothered about the exact time. They lived simply by the sun. They just divided the night up into four parts called *watches*. This word came from soldiers who took turns to 'keep watch' over their camp at night. Each watch lasted about three hours. From six o'clock to nine o'clock was *evening*. From nine o'clock to twelve o'clock at night was called *midnight*. Susanna and her bridesmaids had to be ready by the evening. But Levi and his groomsmen were delayed. They did not come until during the hours of the midnight watch.

The bridesmaids were all ready early in the evening watch. They had cleaned their lamps carefully. They had filled them up with oil, and they had trimmed the wicks. Their lamps were all burning brightly. They were all very excited, of course. They were looking forward eagerly to lighting up the happy procession, and to joining in the joyful wedding-feast. They chatted to each other as they waited, talking and laughing about the happy time ahead. But time went by and Levi had not come. They just had to go on waiting, there was nothing else they could do. More time went by, and still Levi had not come. They began to feel tired and sleepy, for it was getting late now. It was not long before they all dozed off to sleep.

The hours went by and the girls slept. Then, suddenly, during the midnight watch, they awakened with a start. 'The bridegroom is coming!' shouted the door-keeper. 'Wake up! Trim your lamps! Levi and his groomsmen are here!' The girls jumped up quickly. Hurriedly they trimmed their lamps – there was not a moment to lose. They had turned their lamps down, earlier in the evening, so as to save oil. But they had waited so long for the bridegroom that most of their oil had been used up. Their lamps were spluttering and flickering. Soon they would be going out.

Now five of the bridesmaids had been very sensible. All the girls knew that bridesmaids at a wedding had to wait until the bridegroom came. These five sensible girls had come prepared. They had each brought a little container, filled with oil, so that they would be able to refill their lamps if necessary. All they had to do now was to pour in the extra oil. Their lamps were soon burning brightly again. They were all ready to light up the procession.

But the other five bridesmaids were foolish girls. They had not thought of bringing extra oil. Their lamps were going out, and the procession was about to begin. What a terrible disgrace it would be if they could not light up the procession!

The five foolish bridesmaids cried out to the five sensible girls. 'Please share your oil with us,' they pleaded. 'Our lamps are going out. We shan't be able to light up the procession if you don't.'

But the five sensible bridesmaids just had to refuse. 'We dare not share our oil with you,' they said. 'If we did, we should not have enough ourselves for the procession to Levi's house. You had better go and buy some.'

The five foolish bridesmaids hurried off. They would have to wake up the man who ran the oil-shop and get their lamps refilled. What a state they were in! How ashamed they felt!

The happy procession set off for Levi's house, singing as they went. Fortunately, they had the lamps of the five sensible bridesmaids to light their way. The guests were all waiting at Levi's house. As soon as they heard the singing, they hurried out to greet the bride and bridegroom. Then they all went into the house. The door was shut and barred, and the happy wedding-feast began.

Meanwhile, the five foolish bridesmaids had been hurrying to the oil-shop. It had taken time to wake up the owner and to get him to fill all their lamps. Then they had to hurry back to Levi's house. By the time they got there, the feast had been going on for some time. The guests were all having a wonderful time – eating and drinking, laughing and singing and dancing.

The poor girls banged hard at the door. It was some time before their knocking was even heard. How miserable they felt, shut out in the night. They went on banging desperately, hoping that someone would hear them. Then at last came a stern voice: 'Who's that? What do you want?'

'Please, Lord – open the door and let us in!' they cried.

But the door was not opened. 'I don't know you,' came the reply through the closed door. 'All the guests are in here, and the wedding-feast began a long time ago.'

So the five foolish bridesmaids were shut out of the wedding-feast. All they could do was to make their way back to their homes, weeping bitterly in their disappointment.

That fine story of Jesus was also about the Good News that he had brought to earth. He had come to make known the love of God for all his children. He invited men to enter into God's family and to live as his children. Then God would be their heavenly Father.

Sometimes Jesus spoke of God as our King, too. God's kingdom is not like an earthly kingdom. It is in the hearts of those who love him, in return for his love. He rules in the hearts of those who love him and serve him and obey him. Jesus invited men to enter into this Kingdom of God.

Jesus gave this invitation to everyone. Some people heard him gladly and gave their hearts to God. He became their Father and their King. They lived as children of the heavenly Father, as subjects of the heavenly King.

Some people were careless about the invitation. They were like the five foolish bridesmaids. They did not think about it seriously. They did not prepare themselves. They were in danger of being shut out of the kingdom of God, just as the careless girls were shut out of the wedding-feast.

The Good Traveller

Palestine, the land of Jesus, was ruled over by the Romans. It was part of their great empire. Their mighty armies had conquered many lands. All these lands had to be kept at peace and their peoples had to be kept loyal to Rome. Law and order were kept by Roman soldiers. Their legions had to be ready to move quickly to any place where there was a revolt against Rome. That was why the Romans built strong, straight roads, made of layers of stones and raised above the level of the ground, so that rain-water would run off them. They were covered with blocks of limestone, joined together with cement. Roman roads were made strong so that they would last a long time. Some of them can still be seen today.

The Romans made roads for their soldiers in Palestine, too. But they were simply main roads, crossing the country. The Romans did not bother to make roads between towns and villages. Nor did the Jews. Their roads were simply paths or tracks. They did not like travelling. They did not have any carts and they travelled on foot, or on donkeys or asses. These were sturdy animals and they could carry big loads. They were sure-footed and could pick their way over any rough ground.

You can see why the Jews did not bother to make good roads. Only rich and important people had camels or horses. For most people, the tracks were good enough for their donkeys. Sometimes they did make the path level, take away the stones, and fill in the holes. But then the heavy rains came and washed away the ground. In the rainy season these tracks could not be used at all.

Travelling was dangerous. Besides the weather and bad roads there were robbers. They lurked by the wayside, behind rocks, ready to leap out on lonely travellers. Jews travelled together for safety. No one travelled alone unless he had to, for that would be asking for trouble. One of the most famous stories that Jesus told was about a man who travelled alone and, sure enough, he fell into trouble.

A certain Jew named Simon had been on a visit to Jerusalem, to do business there. His home was at Jericho, twenty miles away. When he had finished his business in the great city, he was eager to get back home. Jerusalem was high up, for it is built on hills, but it was hot and dry and dusty compared with low-lying Jericho. In fact, Jerusalem is 3,000 feet higher. That is why the track from Jerusalem to Jericho went downhill all the way.

Jericho was a fine place to live. It was like an oasis among the bleak and barren hills and had a fine climate all the year round. It was famous for all the fruits and plants that grew there. No wonder Simon was eager to get back home again.

Now there was a caravan of people going to Jericho the next day. If Simon had been sensible, he would have waited to go with them. But he just could not wait to get back home. He decided to travel alone.

Simon knew that he was taking risks. The road from Jerusalem to Jericho was only a track between the bare rocks. It was just the place for robbers. They hid behind the rocks, pounced out on unwary travellers, and then vanished into the hills. This track was even called 'the red road', because so much blood had been shed there.

The Romans had built a fort but the road was twenty miles long, and a man could be attacked anywhere. Since before the time of Jesus, even up to modern times, the track from Jerusalem to Jericho has been a dangerous road to travel.

Simon was too impatient to wait. He did not have a donkey, but he was a good walker. He should be back home before nightfall. He had his bag of money tucked safely in his belt. With his staff in his hand, he passed through the city gate and out on to the road to Jericho. It was downhill all the way, so that he should keep up a good, steady pace.

But Simon did not get very far along the road. Suddenly, without any warning, a band of robbers jumped on him. He had no chance to defend himself with his staff. In a moment they had knocked him to the ground and beaten him into unconsciousness. They seized his bag of money. They even took all his clothes. They left him there, bleeding and unconscious and half-dead. If he did not die from his injuries, he would certainly die from exposure to the fierce heat of the sun.

Now it happened that another solitary traveller came along the road, some time later. He was a priest from the Temple at Jerusalem. His whole life was given to God. He helped to lead the worship at the sacred Temple, the house of God. He offered sacrifices to God. He was a holy man.

The priest may have been hurrying to Jerusalem, to take part in an important service at God's Temple. Then, by the roadside, he saw the body of Simon, naked, wounded, and covered with blood. 'He looks as if he's dead,' the priest thought to himself. 'I must be careful not to go near him.' This was because the Jewish religion said that a man was 'unclean', in the sight of God, if he touched a dead body. A man who touched a corpse had to go through washing ceremonies to make himself clean again, and purify himself, before he could take part in the worship of God once more.

Now you can see why the priest would not go near Simon. He would become unclean, if Simon were already dead and he touched him. Then he would not be able to join in the Temple service until he had purified himself.

The priest was a good man, according to the religion of the Jews. He kept every part of the sacred Law of God. But it said nothing about having to help a wounded man who might be dying. He had no religious duty to the man lying by the roadside. His duty was to get to the service and to worship God in his Temple. That was why he did not go near Simon. In fact, he kept as far away from Simon's body as he could in case he became unclean. He passed by, on the other side of the road, and he hurried on his way.

Some time later, another man came hurrying along the road. He was a Levite. The Levites were men of God, too. They got their name from Levi, the founder of their tribe in very ancient times. Every man who came from the tribe of Levi was holy to God. He assisted the priests in the Temple at Jerusalem. Levites looked after the music and the singing at the services. They were holy men, too. People looked up to them, for they lived by the sacred Law of God and they served in his house.

Now this Levite may also have been hurrying to Jerusalem to take part in the service. Then he saw poor Simon, lying by the roadside, half-dead. He was scared, for the robbers might still be near. They might attack him too. It would be foolish to stop and risk his life, when the man was already dying. Besides, he remembered what the Law said about touching a dead body and becoming unclean.

But there was something else the Levite would have remembered, too. The Jews in those days believed that suffering was sent by God. If a man sinned against God, he would suffer for it. If he suffered, then he must have sinned against God. The Jew, lying there in the road, must have committed a dreadful sin against God. His suffering was God's judgment upon him. God was punishing him for his sin. It would be going against God to help him.

The Levite also was a good man, according to the religion of the Jews. He kept every part of the sacred Law of God. He had no duty to help poor Simon. Indeed, his duty was to keep away from the wounded man, so that he could take part in the Temple service and help in the worship of God. He kept as far away from Simon's body as he could. He passed by, on the other side of the road, and he hurried on his way.

Later still, a third traveller came along the road. He was not a holy man. In fact, he was not a Jew at all. He came from Samaria. The Jews had quarrelled with the people of Samaria a long time ago. Ever since, the Jews and the Samaritans had been bitter enemies. The Jews hated the Samaritans. They would not go near them, if they could help it. They would not even travel through the land of Samaria, which lay between Galilee and Jerusalem. It meant that they had to go a long way round, and that made the journey much longer. But they would rather do that than go near the hated Samaritans. They were foreigners and pagans and enemies of the Jews.

Now this Samaritan was a kind man. He knew that the man lying by the roadside was a Jew – an enemy of his people. But he felt no hatred for poor, wounded Simon. He was a man like himself, and he needed help. In fact, the Samaritan felt very sorry for Simon. As soon as he saw him he hurried to help him.

The good Samaritan got off his donkey and untied his horn of oil and his wine-bottle. He knelt beside Simon and lifted his head. He poured a little wine between his lips to revive him. He gently bathed Simon's wounds with his healing oil, and used his wine to stop the bleeding. As Simon slowly came back to consciousness, he gave him sips of wine to quench his thirst. He tore strips off his tunic to make bandages and he bound up Simon's wounds. He had not stopped to think that the robbers might still be near, and might set upon him. All that mattered was to help poor Simon.

When Simon was feeling better, the Samaritan lifted him gently on to his donkey. He supported Simon firmly with his arm. Then they set off down the road, the good Samaritan walking beside his donkey. He was making for the inn, about half-way along the road to Jericho. It was the only inn on the road. He could see that Simon was looked after properly there.

An inn, in those days, was not like one of our hotels. It was just a courtyard with a wall around it. Travellers took their own food and drink, when they went on a journey. They had their own mattress beds, tied on their donkeys, too. They slept in the courtyard, with their animals tethered near by. Rich people could hire one of the small rooms. The innkeeper had to be paid for anything he did.

When they came to the inn, the good Samaritan led his donkey into the courtyard. He hired a room, and made a comfortable bed for Simon with his own mattress. He gave Simon food and drink, and then settled him down for the night. Simon was beginning to feel better already. But it would be a day or two before he would be fit to travel again.

The next morning the kind Samaritan went to the innkeeper and took out his money-bag. 'Here are two silver denarii,' he said. 'I want you to look after my wounded friend until he is fit to travel again. This money will pay for his room and for food and drink. See that he gets everything he needs. As you know, I come along this road regularly. If it should cost more to restore my friend to health, I will pay you the extra money next time I come this way.'

You will remember that the silver denarius was a Roman coin, and that it was a very good day's pay. The money would be enough for Simon to stay at the inn for two or three days. And anyway, the innkeeper knew that he could trust the Samaritan, if Simon's stay should cost more.

When the good Samaritan came to say good-bye, Simon tried to thank him. 'There is no need to thank me,' said the Samaritan. 'We must all help each other, when we can.'

What a shock that story was to the people who heard it! Fancy making a hated Samaritan the hero of the story! And the villains were a holy priest and a righteous Levite!

Jesus told this story to one of the teachers of the sacred Law of God. This *Scribe*, as he was called, was a clever man. He knew every detail of the Law. He wanted to try Jesus out.

'What must I do to please God?' he asked.

'What does the Law say?' Jesus replied.

'It tells us to love God and to love our neighbours.'

'Quite right,' said Jesus. 'Do that, and you will be dear to God.'

'But who is my neighbour?' the Scribe went on. 'How would you answer that?'

The Scribe was being clever. The Jews believed that only other Jews were their neighbours. They did not have to love foreigners and pagans, like the Samaritans, for example. Did Jesus agree with that? Jesus answered him with this story of the good Samaritan who was loving to Simon, a Jew. Then he asked the Scribe a question. 'Now, tell me – which of those three men was a good neighbour to poor Simon? Which one showed love to him – the priest, the Levite, or the Samaritan? Was it one of the Jews, or was it the foreigner?'

The Scribe hated to answer. But he had to, because everyone was waiting to hear what he would say. But he certainly was not going to say the hated word 'Samaritan'.

'The one that was kind to Simon, I suppose,' he muttered.

'You have answered your own question,' Jesus said. 'Now you go and love your neighbour, just as he did. Then you will be close to God.'

The crowd of Jews were shocked by this story. It angered the Scribes and the priests. Jesus had made a mockery of their religion. But he was teaching the Good News of God's love. God loves everyone. That is why we must love everyone. Everyone is our neighbour.